I spy with my little eye
an animal beginning with ....

It's a
GIRAFFE

Facts about giraffes :

1 A giraffe can sleep standing up

2 Giraffes have no vocal chords

3 A giraffe's heart weight about 25 pounds

4 Giraffes have no vocal chords

I spy with my little eye
an animal beginning with ....

It's a

SHRIMP

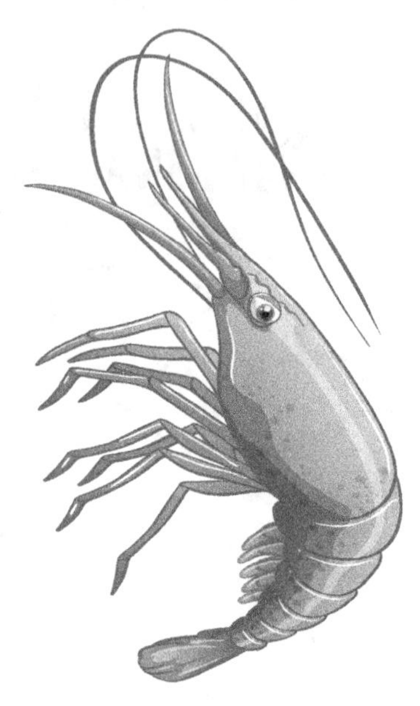

A fact about shrimps :

The heart of a shrimp is located in its head.

I spy with my little eye
an animal beginning with ....

It's a
KOALA

Facts about koalas :

1 Koala fingerprints are so similar to human fingerprints

2 A koala can eat half a day.

I spy with my little eye
an animal beginning with ....

It's a

RHINOCEROS

A Fact about rhinoceros :

A rhinoceros' horn is made of hair.

I spy with my little eye an animal beginning with ....

It's an

ELEPHANT

Facts about elephants :

1   Elephants are the only animal that can't jump

2   Baby elephants suck their trunks for comfort

I spy with my little eye
an animal beginning with ....

It's a PENGUIN

Facts about penguins :

1 Penguins have invisible ears.

2 Penguins have excelent hearing.

3 Nearly three percent of the ice in Antarctic glaciers is penguin urine.

I spy with my little eye
an animal beginning with ....

It's a

FROG

A fact about frogs :

Frogs cannot vomit cause they'll vomit their entire stomachs.

I spy with my little eye
an animal beginning with ....

It's a

PEACOCK

A fact about peacocks :

Only the males are called peacocks.
Females are called peahens

I spy with my little eye
an animal beginning with ....

It's a

CAT

Facts about cats :

1 Cats meow to get attention from humans not for communication

2 Cats can't taste sugar, they don't have sweet buds

I spy with my little eye
an animal beginning with ....

It's a

DUCK

A fact about ducks :

Ducks like to surf

I spy with my little eye
an animal beginning with ....

It's a

SNAIL

A fact about snails :

A snail can sleep for three years

I spy with my little eye
an animal beginning with ....

It's an

OSTRICH

A fact about ostrichs :

An ostrich's eye is bigger than its brain

I spy with my little eye
an animal beginning with ....

It's a

WOLF

A fact about wolves :

Wolves can stay alive without eating for more than a week.

I spy with my little eye
an animal beginning with ....

It's a

KANGAROO 

A fact about kangaroos :

Kangaroos can't fart

I spy with my little eye
an animal beginning with ....

It's a

TURTLE

A fact about turtles :

Turtles can breathe through their butts.

I spy with my little eye
an animal beginning with ....

It's a

BUTTERFLY

A fact about butterflies :

Butterflies taste with their feet

I spy with my little eye
an animal beginning with ....

It's a
cow

Facts about cows :

1 Cows have best friends

2 A cow gives nearly 200,000 glasses of milk in a lifetime.

I spy with my little eye
an animal beginning with ....

It's a

BEAR

A fact about bears :

A bear's bite can crush a bowling ball

I spy with my little eye
an animal beginning with ....

It's a

CLOWNFISH

A fact about clownfish :

All clownfish are born male,
some turn female to enable mating

I spy with my little eye
an animal beginning with ....

It's a

SQUIRREL

A fact about squirrels :

Squirrels plant thousands of new trees each year by merely forgetting where they put their acorns.